9-21-06

D0478919

fast fun & easy®

CHRISTMAS DECORATIONS

Festive Fabric Keepsakes
to Create & Embellish

Linda Johansen

C&T PUBLISHING

Text © 2006 Linda Johansen

Artwork © 2006 C&T Publishing, Inc.

Publisher: Amy Marson

Editorial Director: Gailen Runge

Acquisitions Editor: Jan Grigsby

Editor: Liz Aneloski

Technical Editors: Carolyn Aune and Robyn Gronning

Copyeditor/Proofreader: Wordfirm Inc.

Design Director: Kristy K. Zacharias

Cover Designer: Christina Jarumay

Production Artist: Kirstie L. Pettersen

Illustrator: Tim Manibusan

Production Assistant: Tim Manibusan

Photography: Diane Pedersen and Luke Mulks, unless otherwise noted

Published by C&T Publishing, Inc., P.O. Box 1456, Lafayette, CA 94549

Library of Congress Cataloging-in-Publication Data

Johansen, Linda

  Fast, fun & easy Christmas decorations : festive fabric keepsakes to create & embellish / Linda Johansen.

     p. cm.

  ISBN-13: 978-1-57120-340-3 (paper trade)

  ISBN-10: 1-57120-340-0 (paper trade)

  1. Christmas decorations. 2. Textile crafts. 3. Machine sewing. I. Title: Fast, fun and easy Christmas decorations. II. Title.

  TT900.C4J6155 2006

   745.594'12–dc22

2005034636

Printed in China

10 9 8 7 6 5 4 3 2 1

Acknowledgments

A book is never a solo achievement. I owe so much to so many. The following people (and pets) have kept me sane during this process, and I am eternally grateful to them.

Jay Thatcher—this one was your idea

Jay, Janelle, and Evan—thanks for being such great kids and fine adults

Holly Halley and Gordon Halley—you did a good job

Shady and Mocha—still here all day every day

Kim Campbell and Libby Ankarberg—words can't express my thanks, nor tell how much you contributed to this book

Quilt shop owners, staff, and teachers—I'm humbled by your enthusiasm and good wishes

C&T Publishing folks—especially Liz Aneloski, Carolyn Aune, Diane Pedersen, Luke Mulks, and so many more. Read all the names in the fine print; they are *super* folks to work with, and they are definitely not behind the scenes—they are the scene. None of this would have happened without their support and encouragement.

Contents

Introduction

I think we all enjoy creating our own environment. Challenging ourselves by learning how to make things keeps us active and engaged in life. Combine this challenge with the ability to give inexpensive and individualized gifts and you have the recipe for a holiday to warm the heart. Let the kids help, too. I hope you find the projects rewarding and that you have as much fun with this book as I have had.

In the holiday tradition, all the projects call for embellishment—as much or as little as you like. The ornaments, wreaths, and gingerbread houses can be decorated to your taste. Use them as an excuse (if you need one!) to buy glitzy, unusual fabrics—lamés, silks, satins, polyester shimmeries and iridescents. By taking a bit of extra care with the fusing, you can get a wonderful effect. Many of the projects can be made without even setting up your sewing machine! Spend some time hunting for buttons, beads, and trims—or going through what you have. For even more fun, make the projects with a group of friends.

Choose ornaments for the Advent calendar tree that mean something special to your family or friends. If you start in October and make three or four of the same kind of ornament each day, by December 1 you will have multiple calendars ready to give—just in time to be used. Making a wreath for your front door (or doors!) is a chance to express, with your choice of fabrics, who you are.

For several years our family exhibited in a local gingerbread art show each November. Our best exhibit was the homes of the Three Little Pigs. We each did one of the houses, using wheat cereal for bales of straw, straight pretzels for sticks, and hard candies for bricks. Every year, it was a lot of work making a house and decorating it, only to have it eaten. Now you can make the house of your dreams, then fold it flat and store it away for next year. Then, make a sleigh to sit in the front yard of the house and dream of where it would take you.

The All the Basics chapter is essential to every project in the book, so be sure to read it. It includes specific techniques and more—I guarantee you'll learn some new tricks and tools.

So ... immerse yourself in the glitz and glamour and enjoy personalizing your holiday season.

Happy holidays!

Linda Johansen

all the basics

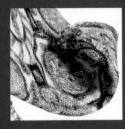

Make it easier—Start here and you won't go wrong! All the Basics will guide you in choosing fun materials, the perfect tools, and helpful techniques. Need extra help? It's in this chapter.

Basic Materials

fabric

There are some wonderful glitzy cotton Christmas fabrics available now that are very easy to use. The ones that attracted me for these projects had lots of glitter, gold, or foil on them. See Resources (page 63) for some specific manufacturers.

I hope you will stretch a bit and also try some of the very lush synthetic fabrics available. I have found that with a bit of patience I can fuse almost anything to any stiff interfacing—and the results are definitely worth it! Always test a sample first. A piece of the backing paper from fusible web used as a protective cloth will disperse the heat well for most applications, and I rarely reduce the iron temperature.

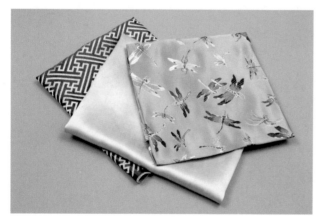

Glitzy fabric can add a lot of fun to your projects.

The Advent calendar (page 54) calls for felt. You can use whatever you like, but I like the homespun look and feel of felt. Yardage is available from many craft and quilt stores. Feel it for thickness and quality. Usually, you will want a good thick, quality felt, but sometimes you will want a thin one for an accent.

interfacing

Timtex and fast2fuse have revolutionized quilting and crafting. They are very stiff interfacings made of rayon and polyester and can be shaped by steaming them and holding them to a shape. Fast2fuse already has fusible web on both sides and makes many of the projects *very* fast, fun, and easy. It comes in regular weight and heavyweight. For some projects, I have specified which interfacing worked best for me. If it isn't specified, any of them will work well.

paper-backed fusible web

If you are using fast2fuse you will use less fusible web, but you will still need it for some of the projects. A number of the projects call for scraps, so hang on to those smaller pieces! Wonder Under has worked the best for me. I find that other types of fusible web gum up my needle and add extra bulk to sew through.

Hang on to the paper backing as well. It is very useful for protecting your ironing board when you fuse small pieces of fabric with scraps of web that aren't quite the same size. It is also useful as tracing paper and as a stabilizer.

thread

Many quilters are reluctant to embrace polyester thread. I have found it to be great fun, a nice look, and easier to use than cotton on many projects.

Some of the projects also call for polyester monofilament thread. This works better than nylon monofilament thread, since it can take the heat of the iron. Superior Threads makes a very nice monofilament in both dark and clear.

glue

Glues that dry clear and soft are best for holding the ends of your sewing threads. If they say they are washable, even better. Aleene's Stop Fraying meets all these criteria. Fray Check works well in places where you won't be sewing over it. Thread Fuse is another option, again if you do not need to sew over it. It does dry hard and can break needles. Aleene's Jewel-It works very well to permanently glue anything to the fabric (or to anything else for that matter!).

fusible powder

Bo-Nash makes a dry powder that can be sprinkled on fabric to fuse it to just about anything you might want. It is especially useful for fusing lace onto the ornaments or other projects. Simply spray the lace lightly with water (over a protective sheet), sprinkle the powder on, lift the lace and place it where you want to fuse it. The water holds the powder to the lace so that there is no fusible available to stick to the iron through the holes in the lace. You can even reuse the excess powder.

template plastic

I have found a plastics shop that caries $\frac{1}{16}''$-thick styrene that I really like. It cuts well and is stiff enough to hold up to my hard use. A 4' × 8' sheet costs about $20, and you can ask to have it cut smaller for you. You may also want to try the thinner clear plastic that quilt stores carry—especially if you will be doing any fussy cutting.

rattail cording

You can use rattail cording to finish the edges of most of the projects if you wish. Rattail is a $\frac{1}{8}''$-thick smooth, woven, round cord made of rayon or nylon. I recommend the rayon for its beautiful shimmery luster. Zigzag it onto the edge for a fast, easy finish. It can also be used to make hanging loops (page 11). See Resources on page 63.

Rattail cording makes finishing the edges a snap.

Basic Supplies

sewing machine

Your machine will need to have straight stitch and zigzag stitch capabilities for many of the sewn projects. Beyond that, some decorative stitches can be fun, but they aren't necessary. Be sure the machine is in good working order.

sewing machine needles

Many of us don't pay much attention to the sewing machine needle. If it works, we are happy. I can't tell you how often in classes, when I ask individuals how long they have had their needles in, they have no idea! If you are having any sort of trouble with your stitches, change your needle. Change it regularly and you will be amazed what a difference it can make in your finished project. I use 80/12 or 90/14 top-stitch needles for almost all my sewing. They are very sharp and have a larger eye and a nice deep slot up the back to protect the thread, so I have very little thread breakage. They work well for cotton, polyester, and monofilament threads.

sewing machine feet

A wide, open-toed embroidery foot allows you to see where the needle is sewing and provides a slot under the foot with room for cording. If you want to do free-motion stitching for embellishing, you will need a darning foot.

stiletto

Find a stiletto that fits your hand well. I like one with a sharp point and a bent tip, so I can slide it under the needle, right where I want the point to hold the cording until the needle catches it. The one I use is actually called a teasing needle and is traditionally used for dissecting. These needles are very inexpensive and can be found at some university bookstores or scientific supply stores.

scissors

I keep several pairs of scissors handy for working on the projects: a sharp pair of 6″–7″ sewing scissors for cutting stiff interfacing and fabrics; a pair of good craft scissors for paper, stencil, and miscellaneous cutting; and, of course, some double-curved, duck-billed embroidery scissors. My new favorite scissors are the Omnigrid 4″ Needlecraft Scissors. They are wonderful for cutting tight curves, cutting windows out, and getting into small places. They are *very* sharp and cut cleanly to the end.

marking tools

For most projects, I use whatever is handy for marking the patterns onto the fabric. If a specific marking tool is required for a particular project, it will be mentioned.

rotary cutting equipment

For these projects, you will likely want a 12½″ square ruler, a 6″ × 12″ ruler, and a small ruler that you can use for things like cutting out the windows on the gingerbread house.

Try flipping your mat over to the unlined side and using only the lines on your ruler. I find this much less confusing—it's easier to see what I am cutting. The newer turning mat by Olfa can save you some time and energy in cutting small pieces.

I strongly recommend the ergonomic cutters that lock easily with the push of a button. If you can easily lock your rotary cutter, you are more likely to do it—after every cut!

One of my favorite tools is the Olfa circle cutter. It makes cutting circles much simpler and speedier. It can be set to cut circles from 1½″ to 8½″ in diameter.

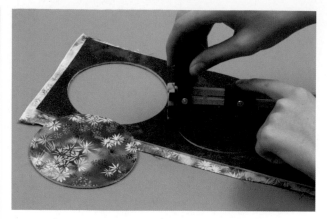

Cut circles quickly and easily with a circle cutter.

ironing equipment

A mini iron is handy to use when the pieces are small, or when you are folding fabric back over the edges of stiff interfacing. Use a larger standard iron for general fusing.

Ironing board protective sheets or freezer paper will keep your ironing board clean and keep stray fusible web off the front of your projects.

Use hot iron cleaner regularly. It will make a big difference in how easy it is to iron small pieces and keep the surface of your projects clean.

Keep your working space and tools clean, and your projects will benefit.

Basic Techniques

stitching

Both sides of the stitching (top and bobbin) will show on many of the ornaments. To make sure you get good tension on both sides, practice your stitches on scraps similar to what you will be sewing on.

marking & cutting

After marking around templates on fabric, cut just inside the lines so the marking doesn't show around the edge of the ornament. This is especially important when using light-colored fabric. It is also important when painting the edge or zigzagging cording on because these finishes don't cover the edge as well as satin stitching does. If you are marking the pattern on stiff interfacing, cutting inside the lines is not a concern.

Be sure to cut out the project just inside the lines, like the one on the right.

fusing for different edge finishes

Several fusing methods can be used for different edge-finish options.

Edge finishes using different fusing methods

Cording or Fabric Paint Edge

1. Lay your fast2fuse (or Timtex, with fusible web on the whole fabric piece) on the ironing board and place your fabric over the stiff interfacing.

2. Fuse the fabric to this first side.

3. Trim the fabric to the edges of the stiff interfacing.

4. Fuse the fabric to the second side.

5. Finish the edges with cording (pages 10–11) or fabric paint.

fast!

You don't need anything under the fast2fuse when ironing the first side of the fabric on. It is thick enough that the heat doesn't transfer.

Fabric Edge

This method finishes the edges with fabric, for a very neat, clean look.

1. Lay your fast2fuse (or Timtex, with fusible web on the whole fabric piece) on the ironing board and place your fabric over the stiff interfacing.

2. Fuse the fabric to this first side.

3. Trim the fabric ½˝ larger than the stiff interfacing.

4. Fold one edge of the fabric to the second side of the stiff interfacing and fuse it down.

5. Fold the second edge of the fabric down and fuse it up to the corner.

Fuse the first side and then the second.

6. Fold the excess corner fabric back one or two times, accordion fashion, to hide it behind. Pin the fabric.

Fold the excess corner fabric accordion fashion and pin it.

7. Fuse a piece of fusible web to the back of another piece of fabric and cut it 1/16″ smaller than the interfacing.

Hold the folds with a stiletto while you iron the back piece on.

8. Carefully center and fuse it to the second side.

9. On sharp corners you will need to keep the corner layers together somehow. You can either glue a bit in the folds or sew around the piece very close to the edge (with monofilament, matching, or contrasting thread) after it is fused.

Sew around the edge to hold the folded corners flat.

attaching rattail cording

1. Use polyester monofilament thread in the needle and bobbin, and a sharp 80/12 top-stitch needle. It will make a world of difference.

2. To begin attaching the cording, widen the zigzag width to 4.0 and do a few stitches in place.

3. Narrow the zigzag to about 2.5 or 3.0 and sew along the edge, just barely catching the edge of the rattail cording. Go slowly around the corners. It pays to take your time.

4. For inside corners, let the needle go over the outside edge of the cording and leave your needle down as you raise the presser foot to turn the corner. This holds the cording close to the corner and anchors it into the corner. Remember, you are not sewing over the outer edge of the cording except at inside corners.

5. For outside corners, go just past the first edge and leave your needle down just inside the cording (and outside the stiff interfacing). This provides a pivot point as you turn the piece and keeps the cording from pulling the corner too round. You may want to twist the cording a bit tighter to keep a crisp corner, but be sure you don't pull on it as you twist it.

 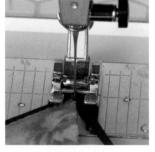

On an inside corner, leave the needle down on the outside of the cording as you go around the corner.

On an outside corner, leave the needle down to pivot around the corner and keep it crisp.

6. Widen the zigzag stitch to 4.0 again to secure the cording at the end. Sew the wide zigzag at the end right up to the starting point so that you can clip the cording end flush with the start.

Clip the cording flush with the thread
at the beginning.

7. Use a drop of thread glue at the start/finish spot. Check the type of glue you are using on a sample piece to be sure it doesn't darken your fabric. Just a little patience helps this process a lot.

shaping & steaming

Both fast2fuse and Timtex can be easily shaped. After the pieces are finished, steam iron them and hold them to the shape you want. This can get hot! It helps to have something like a small glass to hold the warm piece over while it cools, so that you don't burn your fingers.

Shape the project with a solid object after it has been steamed.

hanging methods

Cording or thread—which to use?

☐ Cording will keep the ornament in place so that it will not be able to turn when hanging. Do you want to see only one side?

☐ Cording puts more color on the tree.

☐ Rattail cording may overwhelm some ornaments.

☐ Thread allows for turning.

☐ Thread is not as visible.

Hanging with Cording

1. Begin to zigzag the cording at least a couple of inches away from where you want to put the hanging loop, to give yourself room to work with the loop. Zigzag the cording on (see Attaching Rattail Cording).

2. When you get to where you want the loop, widen the zigzag to 4.0 and stitch completely over the cording to anchor it.

3. Make a large loop, bringing the cording back across itself right next to the ornament. Pull the loop back and anchor this side with a few wide zigzag stitches.

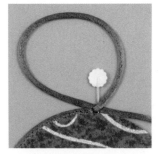
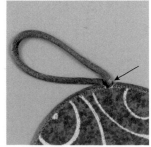

Anchor the first side of the loop and then bring the cording over or under it.

Pull the loop back as you anchor the second part.

4. Narrow the stitch again and finish sewing around the ornament.

Hanging with Thread

1. Thread a needle with a long length (24˝ or so) of thread.

2. Sew through the top of the ornament with the thread doubled. Pull the thread through until you have an even length on each side of the ornament's top. Cut the needle from the thread.

3. Keep the threads even on each side and tie 3 overhand knots next to the ornament to keep the threads in position.

4. Hold one side of the threads, just slightly longer than the other, and tie an overhand knot about 2½"–4" from the ornament. The distance will depend on how low you want the ornament to hang from the branch.

5. Pull firmly on both sides of the threads after you tie the knot to be sure it is tight. I make the two sides different lengths to make it easier to find the center when I'm ready to hang the ornament and to keep the glue away from the pin I use to hang it while it is drying on the design wall.

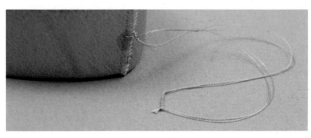

Tie knots next to the ornament and at the top of the thread.

embellishing materials & techniques

One of the most fun aspects of these projects is the embellishing. I've listed below some of the materials I discovered during this process. Please check in the Resources section (page 63) to see where you can find them.

Use your own buttons, lace—anything you can think of! Let me know if you find any really good embellishments and I'll add them to my web page "Tips & Tricks" (www.lindajohansen.com).

Hot-Fix or Iron-On Crystals

These are small sparkly jewels that have a bit of glue on the back. They are great fun when you want to add sparkle to projects and ornaments, and they are very easy to use. I've used them one at a time and in multiples. The glue fuses the crystal to the fabric, or anything else, when heat is applied. All you need is a mini iron or heat wand. Heat wands are special wands with tips that fit the crystals, for easy application (Resources page 63). Other shapes are also available.

1. Put the appropriate tip in the heat wand and plug it in. Be careful to have a clear, safe place to set it while you are working. You can keep a sturdy coffee mug nearby to put the wand in while not in use. I like to use the flat tip so I can apply multiple shapes without having to change tips.

2. Place the crystals where you want them and press gently and squarely on the top for about 10 seconds. More complete instructions come with the

wands. Please read them and follow them carefully to avoid any burn accidents. Be sure to add these crystals on after any machine sewing!

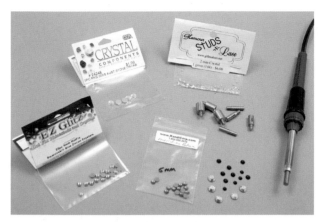

Hot-fix crystals will add sparkle.

Fusible Ribbon

This narrow (⅛″) ribbon is great for small embellishing touches. It can be cut at any angle, overlapped, and fused with your iron, and it comes in lots of great colors. It is wonderful for accents and design elements for many of the projects.

1. To apply long pieces, clip the end you will fuse first to the shape, set it on the project, and then gently run the iron along the piece.

2. Stop just short of where you want to end. Clip the piece to the shape and length you want, and finish fusing it down.

NOTE
When fusing a strip, be careful not to pull the ribbon while you are applying it, since the ribbon will move while the glue on the back is warm.

3. For short pieces, such as the reindeer antlers and snowman nose, clip the ribbon to the shape you want, place it on the ornament, and iron it down. You can hold one end of it in place with a stiletto if needed.

Paint-on Snow

This is available at craft stores, and there are several different kinds. I like the kind that dries white, with flecks of glitter or iridescent plastic in it. I haven't found the clear glitter glue to look as snowlike.

Before applying it be sure you have a good place to dry it. Use a flat toothpick to press it onto the edges of the trees, and then pin the piece to a design wall or the side of a cardboard box with a long pin to let it dry.

3-Dimensional Paint

This paint can be applied to create a dimensional edge line, or it can be smoothed flat so it doesn't add any dimension, but finishes the edge. Tap the bottle upside down a bit before opening, and open it upside down (without squeezing) to eliminate any air bubbles. Practice on a scrap of fabric to see how thick the line will be, and adjust your squeezing and applying speed accordingly.

Hot ribbon, glitter dimensional, and paint-on snow can be used to create great details.

Glue-ons

When you want to add things such as buttons, ribbons, or other embellishments, I recommend Aleene's Jewel-It. This glue holds well and starts drying quickly, so you don't have to hold things in place. It is a permanent bond. Use a smaller amount of glue than you think you need, and have a small rag or paper towel ready to wipe away any glue that you don't want to show. Even though it does dry clear, you don't want big plastic bumps around your decorations.

easy!

Keep a couple of toothpicks handy to put small spots of glue right where you want them. If you wipe them after use, they can be reused. A small plastic bottle lid makes a great safe place to put them down for a moment when necessary.

Beading

You can do your own beading to get just the effect you want (see the All-in-One Beading Buddy by C&T Publishing), or you can buy trims with the beads already strung on them. These trims usually have a narrow woven cotton band that supports the beads. This band can be sewn inside the ornament or between the layers.

Get together with friends and share beads, buttons, embellishments, and a great time!

Fusing Unusual Fabrics

To fuse lace or openly woven fabrics, put an ironing board protective sheet (or a piece of backing paper from the fusible web) on the ironing board and iron a piece of fusible web to the back of your fabric. Cool and pull the fused fabric (with the paper) off the protective sheet. Keep the paper backing on the fused side until you are ready to use it. When you use it, be sure to put a piece of the paper backing over the top to keep your iron clean.

Some of the fabric I used in these projects had small plastic beads glued onto it. To attach this fabric, I fused it from the back side of the fast2fuse. It took a bit of time, a hot iron, and pressure, but I managed not to melt the beads!

Fabric with holographic images needs a protective layer over it when ironing, or you will lose all the sparkle and color. Fuse it lightly on lower heat with paper from fusible web over the top.

fun!

Paper can be fused to the stiff interfacings also—give it a try! I don't recommend it for ornaments that will be steamed and shaped, though.

3-dimensional ornaments

No more broken ornaments or having to put the prettiest ones up where the kids, cats, and dog tails can't get them. These lovely charms will sweeten your tree and simplify your decorating—and they're oh so quick & easy.

What You'll Need for All 3-D Ornaments

- Basic supplies
- Fabric—amount will be specified
- Stiff interfacing—sizes will be specified
- Rattail cording—amount will be specified
- Dimensional paint
- Polyester monofilament or thread to match the ornament
- Thread for hangers
- Rotary ruler with 45° and 60° angles
- Stiletto
- Beading needle
- Hand sewing needle and thimble

Spiral

How can a simple circle become such a fun decoration? Follow these very easy directions and you'll find out! Try it with a couple of scraps of dupioni silk and hang a bead off the end for a real eye-catcher.

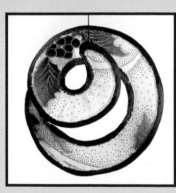

What You'll Need

- 2 pieces of fabric and 1 piece of regular-weight fast2fuse at least 3″ × 3″ each
- 30″ rattail or other decorative cording
- Olfa circle cutter—optional

How-Tos

1. Fuse fabric to both sides of a 3″ × 3″ piece of fast2fuse.

2. Cut a 2½″ circle (or use the pattern on page 28).

3. Trace the pattern onto the fast2fuse and cut it out.

4. Begin zigzagging the cording onto the edge with polyester monofilament thread. (For instructions on sewing around points, see page 10.)

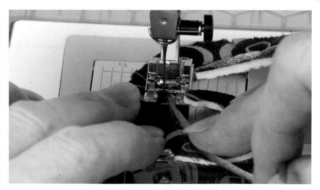

Sew cording on the entire edge.

5. Steam iron the piece when done and shape it to just the spiral you want (page 11).

6. Hang it with a thread (pages 11–12).

easy!

Hang a small bell or sparkly bead from the bottom.

Circle Bell

Two for the time of one! This sweet little bell will charm everyone—especially if you really hang a small jingle bell inside.

You'll Need

- [ ] 1 piece each of 2 different fabrics and 1 piece of regular-weight fast2fuse at least 6″ × 6″ each
- [ ] 26″–28″ rattail cording
- [ ] 2 small jingle bells—optional
- [ ] Embellishments
- [ ] Olfa circle cutter—optional

How-Tos

1. Fuse different fabric to each side of a 6″ round or square piece of regular-weight fast2fuse.

2. Cut into a 5″ circle (or use the pattern on page 28).

A circle cutter makes the job faster and easier.

Cut the circle in half.

3. To cut the circle in half, measure in 2½″ from the edge of the circle and cut a straight line.

4. From this point, you have 2 ornaments to work on. Embellish a different side of each for 2 totally different ornaments—or do the same things to both and have identical ornaments.

fun!

Make the circle a bit bigger and cut it in thirds for a longer, leaner bell.

5. Beginning at the center of the straight cut, zigzag rattail or other decorative cording on using monofilament polyester thread or thread to match your fabric and cording (page 6). Leave about 1″ of cording at the start.

6. At the end, make a loop of cording. Use 6″–8″ of cording, depending on how low you want it to hang. Bring the end of the cording across the start of the loop and anchor it well. Trim the end to about 1″. These ends will be hidden inside the bell.

Leave cording at the start and a loop at the end.

7. Embellish the sides and edges of the bell. Use decorative stitching, hot ribbon, hot-fix crystals, prebeaded fringes, feathers ... go for it!

easy!

Sew some prebeaded fringe inside the bell so just the beads show from the outside. Attach with decorative or monofilament thread, depending on what you want for the outside of the bell.

8. Fold the circle in half and sew the sides together with a 1.5–2.0 width, 1.0 length zigzag (bottom photo on page 19). Backstitch at the start and end. A drop of thread glue at the end will make sure the threads won't pull out. Be careful to keep any embellishment fringes out of the way as you sew up the sides.

9. Steam it a bit (page 11) and gently hold it over the base of a small glass (I finally found a use for that cute shot glass in the back of the cupboard!) to get a nice round shape.

Cool to shape over a small glass after steaming.

fun!

Make the circle bigger, cut it into thirds instead of halves, cut the edge with a wave blade ... play!

Triangular Bell

Three small pieces plus three small holiday bells, and it's a charmer. Listen to its sweet music when the air moves it.

What You'll Need

- ☐ 2 pieces of fabric and 1 piece of regular-weight fast2fuse at least 3″ × 8″ each
- ☐ 30″ rattail or other decorative cording
- ☐ 3 small holiday bells
- ☐ Clearview Triangle Ruler—optional, but very helpful

How-Tos

1. Fuse fabric to both sides of a 3″ × 8″ piece of fast2fuse.

2. Trim the strip to 2½″, and then cut 3 equilateral triangles (pattern on page 28).

3. Zigzag cording around each of the triangles (pages 10–11).

4. Lay 2 triangles back to back and sew them together with a shortened, narrow zigzag (1.5 width, 1.5 length) (see bottom photo below).

5. Lay the third triangle back to back with one of the others and repeat this step.

Sew the 3 triangles together.

6. Fold the piece in half and sew the last 2 sides together. This will mean folding 1 of the triangles in the middle—it's OK! It will easily steam back into shape.

Fold one of the triangles in half to sew the last seam.

7. Thread a long needle with about 30˝ of thread. Double the thread and tie a knot.

8. Insert the needle into the sewn-together point from the inside, then turn around and insert it from the outside through to the inside. (This hides the tail of the knot.)

Insert the needle from the inside of the bell to hide the tails.

9. Thread a bell on and take the needle through the top again. Make a few small anchoring stitches to hold it to the length you want and repeat for the other 2 bells.

10. Hang it with the same thread (pages 11–12). Put a small drop of thread glue at the top to hold all the stitches.

Gift Box

With just a bit of hand sewing you can create this sweet gift box ornament and the ribbon to decorate it.

What You'll Need

☐ 1 piece of regular-weight fast2fuse at least 4½˝ × 4½˝

☐ 1 piece of fabric 5½˝ × 8˝

☐ Approximately 1 yard of ⅛˝-wide ribbon

☐ Small bow

How-Tos

1. Cut six 1½″ × 1½″ squares of fast2fuse (pattern on page 28).

2. Cut a 5½″ × 8″ piece of fabric into six 2½″ × 2½″ squares.

3. Center one fast2fuse square on a square of fabric and fuse it on. Do not fuse fabric to the second side.

4. Fold over the edges to the back and fuse in place. (Steps 1–6, pages 9–10)

5. With a fagoting stitch or zigzag, stitch the squares together by machine, ready to fold into a box. Use polyester monofilament thread or thread to match your fabric.

6. Sew the remaining edges together by hand. Use an overcast stitch or sew an invisible stitch catching each side alternately. Sew a few anchoring stitches at the end of each seam.

7. Wrap with ⅛″ ribbon, tie a bow, hang by a corner with a thread (pages 11–12), and it's ready to make your tree more festive.

fun!

Make your own bow! Take a 12″ length of ⅛″ ribbon. Mark ½″ from the end, then lightly mark every inch, leaving ½″ at the end. Thread a needle with a single thread and knot it. Thread the ribbon on it going through it back and forth at each mark. Pull the thread tight. Spread the folds out a bit and thread a large bead on, then sew back through it. Sew through 2 more times, catching the bead each time. Sew a few anchoring stitches and glue the ribbon onto your package.

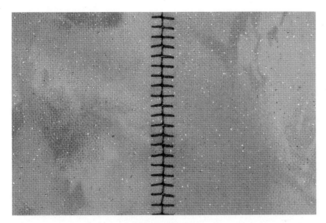

Fagoting stitch

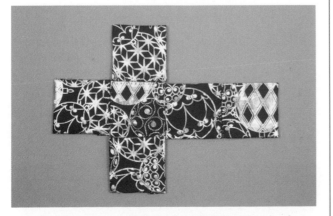

Sew the squares together, ready to shape into a box.

Circle Strip

You can't get much more basic than a straight strip of stiff interfacing and fabric. This is a very fast ornament to make, and with the right fabric and a few beads, it is sure to become a classic on your tree.

What You'll Need

☐ 2 pieces of fabric and 1 piece of regular-weight fast2fuse, at least 2" × 11" each

☐ 20" rattail or other decorative cording

☐ Beads or bells to hang inside the circle

How-Tos

1. Cut a 1½" × 10" piece of fast2fuse.

2. Fuse fabric to both sides of it. Trim the fabric even with the edges of the fast2fuse.

fun!

Open mesh makes a great "fabric" too. Remember to use a protective sheet when fusing it.

easy!

Fuse a strip of fabric that is at least 3" wide to one side of the stiff interfacing, fold the fabric around the long edge, and iron it to the other side. Zigzag cording onto the unfinished long side only.

3. Zigzag cording onto both of the long sides. Be sure to secure it well at the ends. A bit of thread glue helps here (page 10).

Sew the cording to both long sides of the sandwich.

4. Steam iron the strip and pull it around into a circle (page 11). Hold the ends overlapped by about 1˝ while it cools.

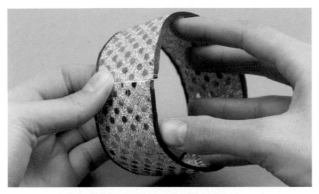

Hold it in a circle while it cools.

fun!

Pull it a bit oval when you shape it. This will frame the beads quite differently.

5. Butt the short ends up to each other, slide them under the presser foot, and zigzag them together. Use at least a 4.0 width and 1.0 length. This stitching can be done with monofilament thread or thread that matches your fabric.

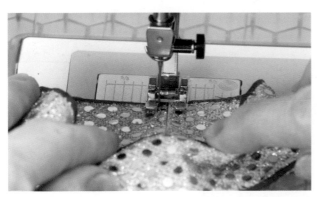

Sew the ends together with a wide shortened zigzag stitch.

6. String some beads (or use prestrung ones like the sample) and hang them from the center of the seam. A bit of glue will hold the ends of all the beading and hanging threads.

7. Hang with a thread (pages 11–12).

Closed Diamond

Use a shimmery fabric, and this diamond will sparkle and shine anywhere in your home.

What You'll Need

- ☐ 2 pieces of fabric and 1 piece of regular-weight fast2fuse at least 2˝ × 9˝ each

- ☐ 30˝ rattail or other decorative cording

- ☐ Beads or bells to hang from the bottom

- ☐ Beading needle or regular needle thin enough to sew twice through your chosen beads

- ☐ Rotary ruler with a 45° angle (or use pattern on page 28)

How-Tos

1. Fuse the fabric to both sides of a 2″ × 9″ piece of fast2fuse.

2. Cut out three 1½″ 45° diamonds (pattern on page 28).

3. Zigzag rattail or other decorative cording around each of the diamonds (pages 10–11). Start and finish on a side rather than at a point.

4. Hold 2 diamonds, insides together, and sew up the side with thread that matches your decorative cording. Stitch them together by hand with a rather large running stitch. You can sew this by machine, but the sides stay smoother if they are sewn by hand.

5. Open the diamonds out, lay the third diamond inside to inside with one of the sewn ones, and repeat Step 4.

Sew the last 2 sides together by hand.

7. Using a beading needle, thread a few beads on a long thread. Thread through them once, go around the last bead, and come back through them. Take the thread out of the beading needle and pass both threads through the eye of a sturdier sewing needle to attach the beads to the ornament. Sew several anchoring stitches and use a drop of glue to hold the stitches.

Hold 2 diamonds together and sew the sides by hand.

6. Open the diamonds up gently and sew the last side together. Sew several extra stitches at the end to pull it in a bit tighter.

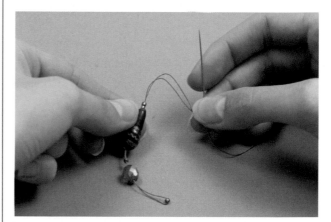

Thread the beads before you attach them.

8. Hang the ornament with thread from the other end (pages 11–12).

For an entirely different look, sew only the top half of the diamonds together, use steam to curl the bottom points outward, and hang a bell or 3 from the inside center.

Open Diamond

What You'll Need

- ☐ 2 pieces of fabric, 1 piece of regular-weight fast2fuse, and 1 piece of fusible web at least 3″ × 11″ each
- ☐ 3 jingle bells
- ☐ Rotary ruler with a 60° angle (or use pattern on page 28)

How-Tos

fun!

Make this one with either 45° or 60° diamonds.

1. Cut three 60° diamonds 1¾″ (pattern on page 28) from a 2″ × 9″ piece of fast2fuse.

2. Lay these fast2fuse diamonds on a piece of fabric, allowing 1″ between each diamond. Cut the fabric into diamonds ½″ larger all around than the fast2fuse.

3. Fuse the fabric diamonds to one side of the fast2fuse.

4. Fold over the edges to the back of each diamond and fuse (pages 9–10).

5. Iron fusible web to a 2″ × 9″ piece of fabric

6. Cut 3 diamonds, ¹⁄₁₆″ smaller than the fast2fuse pieces, from this fabric.

7. Carefully center and fuse these to the second side of each diamond.

8. Use a straight stitch to sew about ¼″ from all the edges of each diamond using monofilament polyester thread. You can sew closer to the edges as long as you catch the piece fused onto the back. The sewing flattens the folded corners.

9. Lay 2 of the diamonds with insides together and sew just the top half with a 1.5 length, 1.5 width zigzag (bottom photo, page 19). Backstitch at the beginning and end.

Sew the 3 diamonds together on one edge only.

10. Repeat this for the remaining 2 sides. The last seam will require folding one diamond in half.

11. Steam the sides and hold them together at the bottom while they cool.

12. Add some tiny jingle bells to hang from each corner and hang with a thread (pages 11–12). For a more open bell, curl the points up instead of under by steam ironing the points and tacking them to the sides with thread or glue.

Folded Star, or Circle, or...

Make this fun three-sided ornament from any shape you like.

What You'll Need

- ☐ 6 pieces of fabric and 3 pieces of regular-weight fast2fuse at least 4″ × 4½″ each
- ☐ Dimensional glitter paint or rattail cording

How-Tos

1. Fuse fabric to both sides of 3 pieces of fast2fuse.

fun!

Cover each side with a different fabric.

2. Trace and cut out 3 stars (pattern on page 28).

3. Sew rattail cording around the edges of all 3 stars (pages 10–11). Dimensional paint will finish the edges well also.

easy!

Fuse fabric to only one side of the fast2fuse. Sew rattail cording around the edges and fuse the 3 together—or cover the edges with dimensional glitter paint after they are fused.

4. Sew 2 stars together at each point on one side only, and in the valley at the bottom with a 3.0 width, 1.5 length zigzag stitch or by hand. Match the edges as carefully as possible.

Sew 2 stars together at each point.

5. Open the 2 stars and fold one of them in half to attach the points of the third star.

Fold one star in half to sew the points of the third star.

6. Fold back the 2 sewn sides and sew the remaining points. Pin as necessary to keep the edges together.

7. Steam the piece to shape if you want the sides to stay close together.

fun!

For a tighter star, use matching or polyester monofilament thread and sew the whole side with a narrow zigzag stitch. You don't even need fabric on the back side.

8. Hang it with a thread (pages 11–12).

fun!

Add some beads or bells at the bottom.

easy!

Cut 3 circles and sew them the same way. This gives a very different look, and the ornament is just as easy to make (folded circle ornament).

For a variation draw a triangle and arc the sides inward to make a more spiky ornament. (folded arced triangle ornament)

PLAY a little bit each day and you'll SOON have enough ornaments for a whole tree!

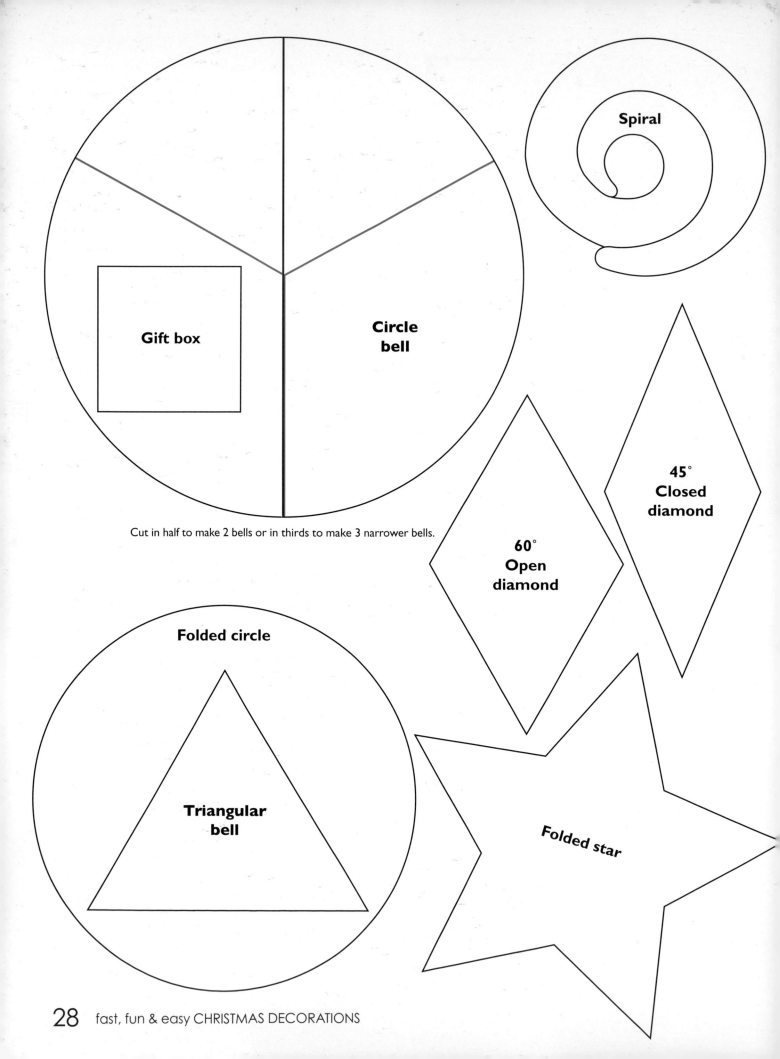

Spiral

Gift box

Circle
bell

Cut in half to make 2 bells or in thirds to make 3 narrower bells.

45°
Closed
diamond

60°
Open
diamond

Folded circle

Triangular
bell

Folded star

wreath

Greet your guests with homemade holiday spirit before you even open the door. Make it this weekend, in your own style and colors!

What You'll Need

- Basic supplies
- Regular-cut ¼ yard of fabric for base
- 6 pieces of fabric 7½″ × 19″ each for leaves
- 1 yard regular-weight fast2fuse
- 5½″ × 18″ fusible web

- 12 yards rattail cording (approximately 16″ per leaf)
- Glue (I recommend Jewel-It)
- Approximately 20 buttons for the berries
- ¾″ or 1″ plastic ring (for café curtains or tieback hooks)

How-Tos

base

1. Cut a 6″ × 36″ piece of fast2fuse.

2. Place this next to the edge of the ¼-yard piece of fabric and fuse.

3. Trim the fabric to the edge of the fused piece on only one long and one short side to neaten.

4. Apply 1¾″ strips of fusible web to the fabric on the other 2 sides.

easy!

When patching fusible web, fuse the first piece to the fabric, then pull up the edge a bit and slide the next piece under it. Iron it back down over the new piece. This keeps fusible off the iron and makes it easy to remove the paper.

5. Trim the fabric on the remaining 2 sides 1½″ from the edge of the fast2fuse.

Wreath base ready to fuse together

6. Remove the paper backing on the long edge only, then gently fold the whole piece in half lengthwise (don't crease it) and fuse the fabric edge over to form a tube.

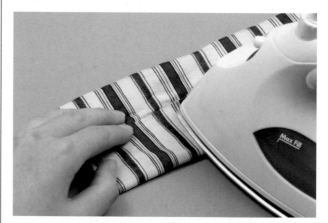

Fold the piece in half and pull the fused fabric over the edge of the fast2fuse and fabric to fuse it.

7. Take the paper off the end. Pull both ends of the tube together and fit the clean-cut end inside the end with extra fabric.

8. Fuse the fabric to hold the ends together. Don't worry about it looking neat and tidy—it will be covered with leaves.

With the clean-cut edge inside, fuse the ends together.

9. Holding the iron over the whole tube, press it lightly and steam iron it. Pull it out to a circle shape and hold it for a bit until it cools. You can reshape it as many times as needed until you get a circular shape. Press down on the whole piece with the steam iron after it is a circle to scrunch it flatter. You can use a large book or weighted cookie sheet to hold it flatter while it cools.

leaves

1. Cut 6 pieces of fast2fuse 3½″ × 19″.

fun!

Make it yours—cut more or fewer leaves to make a more or less full wreath.

2. Cut 6 pieces of fabric 7½″ × 19″.

3. Fuse one side of the fast2fuse to the fabric, lining it up along one edge of the fabric.

4. Fold the fabric over snugly and fuse it to the other side of the fast2fuse.

5. Trace and cut four 60° diamonds (page 28) or 4 leaf patterns (page 34) from each strip.

Cut diamonds out of the strips.

6. If you don't want to trace the leaf pattern, randomly cut small arcs out of the sides of the diamonds to shape them as leaves.

Cut small arcs out of the sides of the diamonds to shape the leaves.

7. Cut a dart up the center of a leaf (pattern on page 34).

Cut a dart and sew up the center of each leaf.

8. Gently pull it together and sew it with a satin stitch. Begin at the top of the dart and sew with a 4.0 width, 0.2 length stitch to the bottom. (This width and length may vary slightly according to your machine. Be sure to test your stitch on a separate piece of fast2fuse.) The zigzag stitch should evenly catch both sides of the dart.

NOTE

After the halfway point (the widest part) of the dart is sewn, you will need to gently pull the edges apart so that they just butt up against each other. They should not overlap.

easy!

Couch some 18 or 20-gauge wire up the center back of the leaves to make them bendable.

fun!

Start the satin stitching very narrow before the dart starts and increase it until it is 4.0 wide, enough to hold the dart together.

easy!

Add some veins on either side of the leaves. Start near the edge of the leaf with a narrow satin stitch and widen it to almost the same width as the main dart as you get close to the main dart.

fun!

Use polyester monofilament thread to sew the dart and then cover it with dimensional glitter glue. You can add extra glitter glue veins, too.

9. Repeat the dart on each leaf.

10. Use polyester monofilament thread to apply rattail cording around each leaf (pages 10–11).

assembly

1. Pin the leaves together in groups of 2, 3, or 4 and pin them to the wreath base. Put a second pin through all the leaves in each group to keep them from sliding around. Move the groups around until you get an arrangement that you like.

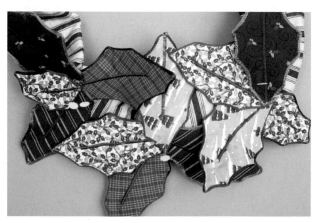

Pin the leaves around the base in groups.

2. Carefully hold the leaves in the position that you want, remove them from the wreath, and slide them under the presser foot of your machine.

3. Using monofilament polyester thread, sew them together at the base of the leaves with a 4.0 width, 1.5 length zigzag stitch. Sew 2 different spots or a short line (½″) of stitching. This stitching will not show. If you don't have monofilament (get some—it's

worth it!), use a thread that closely matches the leaf fabric. Sew one set of leaves at a time and repin them back in the same position on the wreath before you pick up the next group.

easy!

You can glue the leaves together instead of sewing them. Just be sure not to glue the pins into the bouquet!

easy!

Take a digital photo of the wreath and reference it to be sure to get the arrangement you like.

4. Gently lift the edge of each set of leaves and generously apply glue to a spot where the leaves rest on the base.

5. Let the glue dry completely and then pull the pins out.

6. Arrange and glue on some buttons for the berries. These will look better if all the button groups are not the same.

fun!

Thread the buttons with a thicker thread or crochet yarn, tie the thread on the back and fasten with a drop of a thread-fuse product or glue, clip the thread ends short, and glue the buttons on the wreath. It will look like you sewed them on.

7. Sew a small ¾″ or 1″ plastic ring on the back where you want the top of the wreath to be.

Sew a small plastic ring on the back to hang the wreath.

8. Hang the wreath inside or outside (protected from the weather) and you're ready for company!

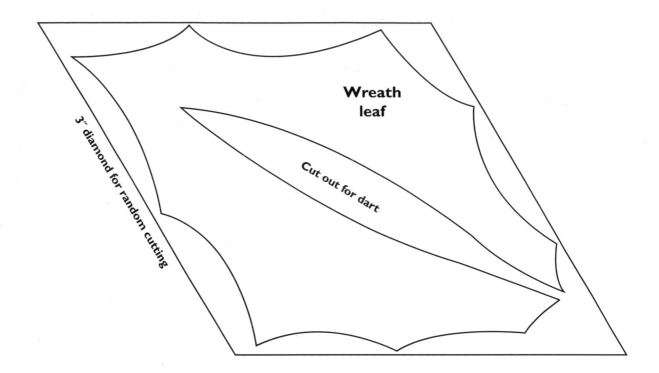

Wreath leaf

3" diamond for random cutting

Cut out for dart

Variations

A. For a different look, make the base and leaves a bit smaller, use some beautiful batik and hand-dyed fabrics, and add fewer leaves so the base shows through more.

B. If it fits your home better, try using some homespun plaids and stripes and add leaf veins.

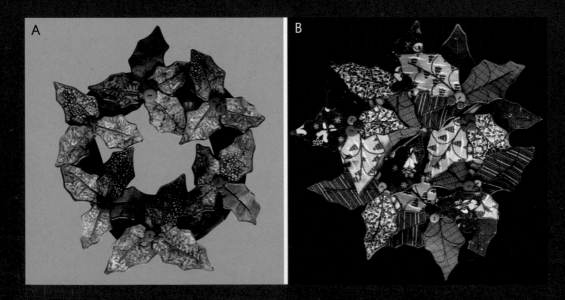

A

B

gift boxes

We all know that some of the best gifts come in small packages—especially when the package is part of the gift. Make several of these for a sweet way to give more than a gift.

What You'll Need

- ☐ Basic supplies
- ☐ Heavy or regular-weight fast2fuse–small box: 5″ × 8″; medium box: 6″ × 9″; large box: 8″ × 12″
- ☐ 2 pieces of fabric–small box: 6″ × 9″ & 8″ × 14″; medium box: 7″ × 10″ & 9″ × 15″; large box: 9″ × 12″ & 9″ × 20″
- ☐ Rattail cording
- ☐ Dimensional glitter paint
- ☐ Polyester monofilament or thread to match the ornament

How-Tos

Box sizes:			
	Small	**Medium**	**Large**
Base	1½″ × 1½″	2½″ × 2½″	3″ × 4½″
Sides	1½″ × 1½″	2½″ × 2″	1″ × 3″ and 1″ × 4½″
	(Cut 4)	(Cut 4)	(Cut 2 of each size)
Lid	1¾″ × 1¾″	2¾″ × 2¾″	3¼″ × 4¾″
Lid sides	¾″ × 1¾″	¾″ × 2¾″	½″ × 3¼″ and ½″ × 4¾″
	(Cut 4)	(Cut 4)	(Cut 2 of each size)

making the pieces

1. Cut all the fast2fuse pieces for the size of box you want to make.

2. Center each piece on fabric that is at least ½″ larger all around and fuse in place.

All the pieces needed for the medium box

3. Trim the fabric ½″ from the fast2fuse. (On the lid sides for the large box, trim the fabric to ⅜″.)

4. Fold the fabric over onto the back of the fast2fuse and fuse in place (Steps 1–6, pages 9–10).

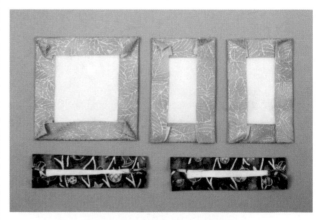

Fuse the edges to the back on all the pieces.

5. Fold the layered corner fabric back on itself so that the fused fabric for the back covers it.

6. Apply fusible web to a piece of fabric—small box: 6″ × 9″; medium box: 7″ × 10″; large box: 9″ × 12″.

7. Cut one piece of fabric with fusible web on the back for each box piece. Cut these pieces 1/16″–1/8″ smaller overall than the box pieces. (For example, a 2½″ square piece would be cut to 2 7/16″ square— just under 2½″.)

8. Take the paper off the back of one piece at a time and iron it to the back of the box piece it matches. Lay it on one edge and iron that edge first. Gently lay it across the whole piece and fuse it down. Often it will stretch a bit—just trim the last edge to fit before you fuse it down completely.

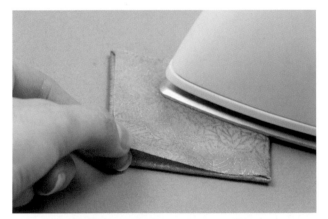

Lay the fusible-backed piece on the back and iron it on.

easy!

To get fusible web paper off easily, gently attempt to tear the edge of the fused piece. The paper will tear and the fabric won't.

assembly

1. Sew the box side pieces to the base with a fagoting or zigzag stitch. Add the sides one at a time, sewing right around the base. Use polyester monofilament thread.

2. Fold the box in half across the base and sew the 2 opposite sides together with a narrow (2.0 width, 1.5 length) zigzag stitch. The needle should catch the fabrics on the left side and go completely off the fabrics on the right side. Remember to backstitch at the start and end of each side seam.

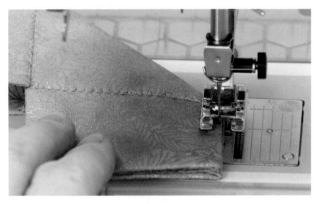

Fold the box in half to sew the side seams.

3. Fold the box to match sides for the third corner. You will need to scrunch the box a bit to do this. It's OK. It will steam back to shape. Repeat for the last corner.

4. Sew the lid sides onto the top and at the corners in the same way that you did the box base.

5. Steam the base and top to shape.

6. Embellish the top. Put a line of dimensional glitter glue around the top edge, glue or sew something special on top, or …

Put a **special** gift in it and know that the **box** will be **treasured** and reused for years.

gingerbread
house

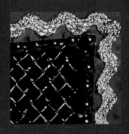

Have a party! Grab your glitz, get together with some of your friends, and let the ideas multiply. This gingerbread house won't supply a year's allowance of sugar, plus you can fold it away to bring out again next year.

Made by Kim Campbell.

What You'll Need

- ☐ 1 yard (large) or ⅔ yard (small) heavyweight fast2fuse (includes base and trees)
- ☐ 1 yard (large) or ½ yard (small) fabric for house
- ☐ ½ yard (large) or ⅜ yard (small) fabric for base
- ☐ 1 fat quarter or scraps of fabrics for trees
- ☐ 2 yards fusible web
- ☐ 2 ¾ yards rattail cording (add approximately 1 yard for each large tree and ⅔ yard for each small tree if putting cording around the trees)
- ☐ 1 yard beaded ribbon trim
- ☐ Small pieces of lace or metallic netting for the windows
- ☐ Embellishing fabric, trims, paints, and more (your imagination is the limit)

How-Tos

cutting & fusing

1. Trace and cut 2 sides and 2 ends for the large (or small) house (patterns on pages 46–48) from fast2fuse. Cut 2 rectangles 5½″ × 10″ for the roof of the large house (2 rectangles 4¼″ × 8½″ for the small house).

2. Place each piece on fabric that is at least ¾″ larger all around and fuse in place.

3. Trim the fabric edges to ⅝″ larger all around than the fast2fuse.

Trim the fabric edges to ⅝″ from the fast2fuse.

4. Fold the fabric over onto the back of the fast2fuse and fuse in place.

5. Iron fusible web to the back of a 16″ × 22″ (large) or 14″ × 19″ (small) piece of fabric.

6. Cut one piece of fabric with fusible web on the back for each section of the gingerbread house. Cut the pieces 1/16″ smaller than the pattern pieces.

7. Iron these to the back of each house section to cover the ironed-over edges.

8. Trace the doors and window on the back side (inside the house) of each house section (patterns on page 46–48). Remember to reverse their locations on one side of the house, depending on whether and where you want the second door. Cut out the doors and windows. Cut most of the lines with a rotary cutter and the corners with small, sharp scissors. Save these pieces!

Cut the corners of the windows with small, sharp scissors.

assembly

1. Sew cording around the inside of all the windows and all the door openings. (See page 10 for more information about sewing the cording around the inside corners.)

2. Cut off ³⁄₁₆˝ from the top and ¼˝ from 1 side of each door you saved from Step 8 (page 39). Then add cording to 3 sides of each door with a fagoting stitch. You do not need cording on the bottom, finished edge of the door.

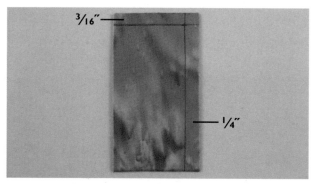

Mark and trim the end and side of the door before adding cording.

fast!

Instead of adding cording, don't trim the doors, and paint the edges with dimensional paint. Match the paint color to the house color, and remember to paint the edges of the door pieces you cut out as well. Let them dry completely.

fun!

To deck your halls with extra glitz, paint the edges and substitute beaded trim for cording around the windows.

3. Sew the doors back on with a fagoting stitch (page 21).

4. Sew one house side to each house end. Use a fagoting stitch to sew all joining seams so that they can fold easily. (A zigzag will work if you don't have a fagoting stitch on your machine.)

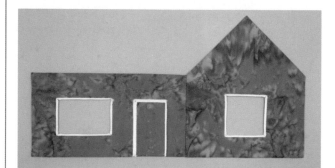

Sew the sides to the ends.

5. Zigzag cording over the joined edges. Trim the ends of the cording and use a drop of thread glue to hold them. Hold the project and glue over something other than your lap. The thread glue sometimes drips.

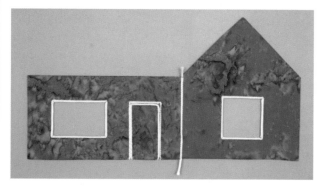

Sew cording over the joined seams.

6. Sew the joined side/end pieces together.

7. Sew cording on this joined seam as well.

8. Sew cording to the 2 ends of the strip of house pieces at this point. Don't sew the last corner together until you have embellished the windows from inside.

This house is ready for embellishment.

9. Sew the roof pieces together along one long side with a fagoting stitch.

10. Zigzag cording over the top of the joining seam. Set it up and try the roof on—I know you are dying to see how it will look.

chimney

1. Cut the chimney pieces (patterns on page 47) from the window pieces you saved in Step 8 under Cutting & Fusing (page 39).

2. Sew the pieces together with a fagoting stitch.

Sew the chimney pieces together.

3. Zigzag cording over the top of the joining stitches and trim the ends. Use a drop of thread glue to hold the ends. Be sure to use a glue that dries soft.

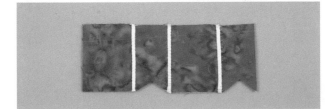

Add cording over all the joined seams.

4. Zigzag cording around the whole strip of pieces.

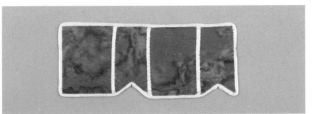

Zigzag cording around the whole piece.

finishing

When you are finished embellishing the house and chimney (pages 43–45), carefully fold them in half and zigzag the open edges together with a narrow zigzag (1.5 length, 2.0 width).

Sew the open edges together after the embellishing is done.

Variation: Add a bit of snow around the top edge of the chimney, set it on the roof, and it's ready for Santa! If you will be storing the chimney flat, remember to allow for folding when you add the snow.

Add a bit of snow to the top of the chimney.

trees

Everyone needs a few trees in the yard...

1. Fuse fabric to both sides of a piece of fast2fuse 4¼″ × 6″ (small tree) or 5½″ × 6½″ (large tree).

2. Trace and cut out 2 trees (patterns on page 48).

3. Cut a slot in each half as shown on the pattern. One slot will extend from the bottom to just a hair beyond the middle, and the other will extend from the top to just a hair beyond the middle.

4. Paint the center slot edges with dimensional paint applied sparingly. Smooth the paint flat so the slots fit together. Let dry.

Finish the slots with dimensional paint applied thinly.

5. Zigzag cording around each half of the tree (starting and finishing at the edges of the slots) (pages 10–11). If you want to paint the edges with dimensional paint or snow, leave space for the tree half that's slotted on the top to slide up to the top of the piece slotted on the bottom. Let the snow or paint dry thoroughly.

6. Slide the 2 halves together and stand the tree up.

base

Hmm, something to set it on...

1. Cut two 8″ × 14″ pieces of fast2fuse (one piece 11″ × 12½″ for the smaller house).

2. Fuse them to a piece of fabric cut ¾″ wider on all sides.

3. Fuse the edges of the fabric over to the back (pages 9–10).

4. Apply fusible web to 2 pieces of fabric the same size as the fast2fuse. Trim this to ¹⁄₁₆″ smaller than the fast2fuse pieces.

fun!

Make the 2 sides of the base different so that you can create 2 different scenes.

5. Fuse the fabric to the back side of the base pieces.

easy!

If you want the base extra stiff, use 2 layers of fast2fuse and cover it the same way. Allow 1″ for folding over to the back and pull it snugly as you iron it.

6. For the large base, sew the 2 pieces together with a fagoting stitch. If you have room to store a larger piece, you can construct it as one piece. The 2 pieces are sized to be able to fit into a box for storage.

Embellishing Ideas

There are no limits to how you can embellish and personalize your gingerbread house. Just be sure you don't get carried away and make the roof too heavy for the walls to hold up!

shingles

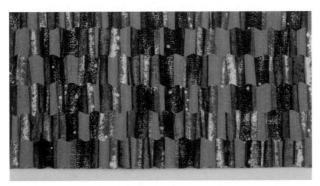

Put wavy-cut fusible strips for shingles on the back side of the roof so you can change it from year to year.

1. Apply fusible web to the back of an 11″ × 12″ piece of striped fabric with the stripes running parallel to the short side.

2. Cut 1″ strips parallel to the long side with a wave blade in your rotary cutter.

3. Overlap the waves, starting from the bottom edge of the roof.

fun!

Use 2 different fabrics and cut them in random lengths for a fun stripy look.

icicles

Sew beaded ribbon to the underside of the eaves for icicles.

1. Sew the ribbon onto the underside of the roof before fusing the back piece of fabric on, or sew it on after—it's your choice. Keep the edge of the ribbon as close as possible to the edge of the roof so that the beads hang freely.

Sew the ribbon as close to the edge as you can.

2. Sew some rickrack on top of the roof, over the sewing line from the beaded ribbon.

Cover the stitching with some rickrack.

window lace
or windowpanes

Fuse shimmery fabric, netting, or lace on the window for a realistic look. Do this before you sew the walls of the house together.

Add lace or windowpanes to windows from the inside, before you sew the walls together.

1. Center and fuse ⅜"-wide strips of fusible web, 1" wider than the window, along each side of the window on the inside of the house. You only need it along the top for lace that will hang as a curtain.

2. Trim the fabric to ½" larger than the window all around.

Iron fusible web around all the windows.

easy!

Pull up the corners of the side strips of fusible web and lay the top and bottom strips under the paper. Iron over all the paper.

3. Peel the paper off one window at a time and carefully lay the fabric over the opening.

4. Fuse the bottom edge of the fabric. You may need a protective sheet for this step, depending on your fabric. You can also use the paper backing from the fusible web.

5. Tug just enough to keep the fabric taut and iron up the sides and across the top edge of the window.

Place the fabric front side down and fuse on one side first.

6. Repeat for all the windows.

wreath

Add yarn for a wreath on the door and a bead for a door handle.

snow

Drape some batting, ostrich feather, or boa trim around the house for snow.

tree decorations

Dot the tree with glitter dimensional paint or glitter glue to suggest ornaments.

Variations

Put your heart into this gingerbread house and it will become a family heirloom.

A. Make the smaller version in gray fabric for a stone house look. Fuse glitzy fabric to the roof to bring it out of the Stone Age.

B. For a more woodsy house, add shingles drawn on the roof with dimensional paint, small sticks around the windows, a moose in the window, and a cat at the door. Made by Libby Ankarberg.

C. Make your own snow by mixing clear, white, and silver beads with a bit of Jewel-It glue.

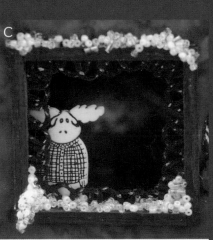

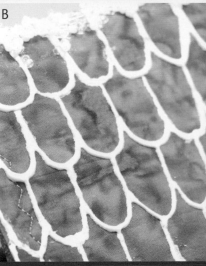

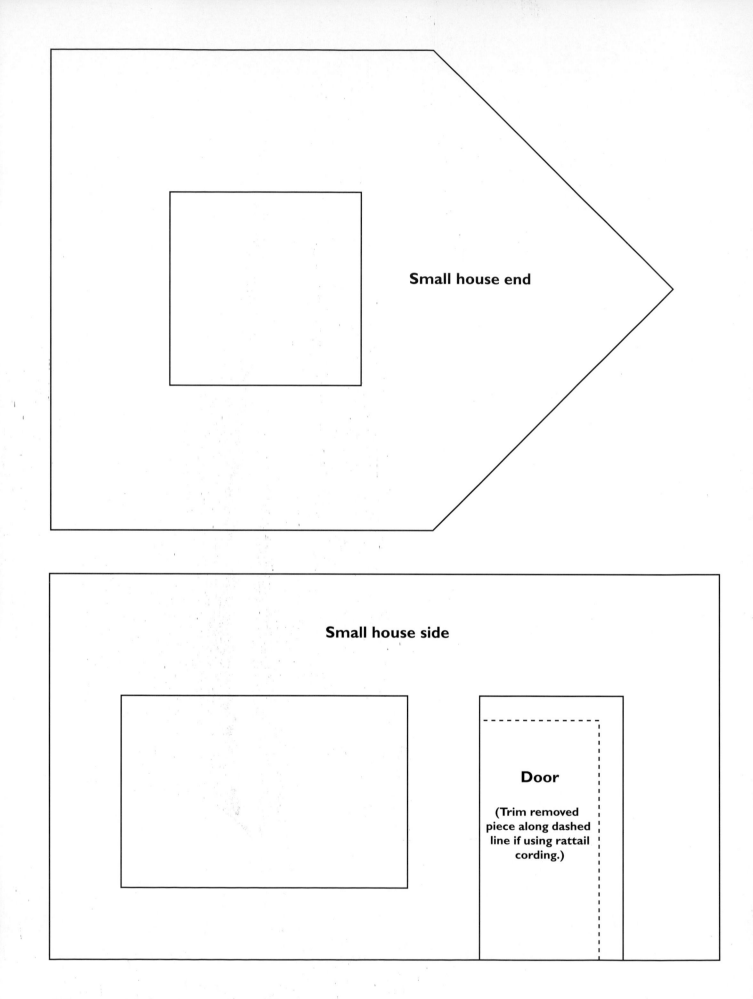

Small house end

Small house side

Door

(Trim removed piece along dashed line if using rattail cording.)

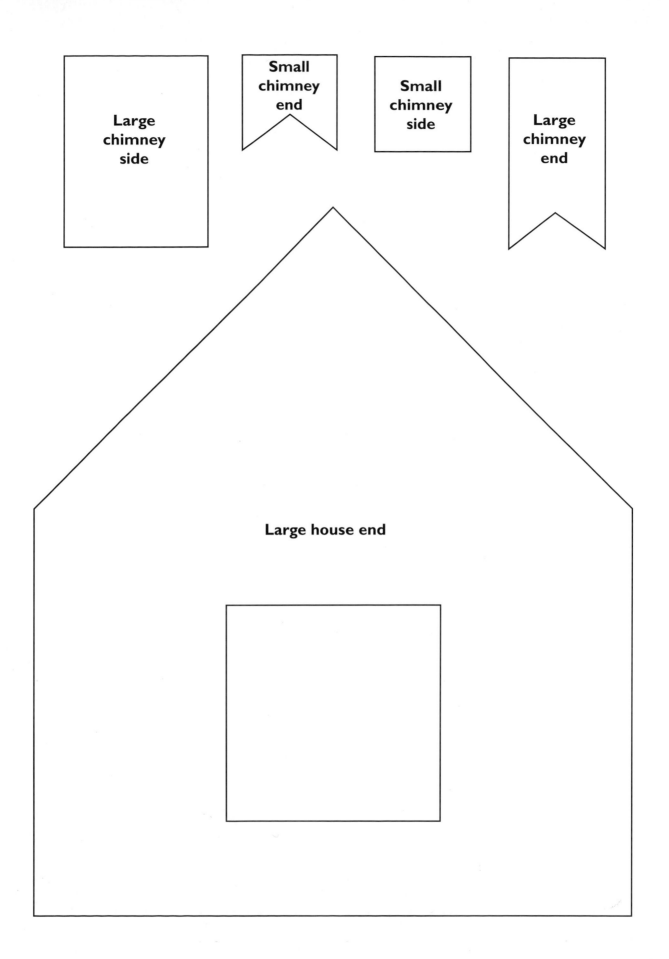

Large chimney side

Small chimney end

Small chimney side

Large chimney end

Large house end

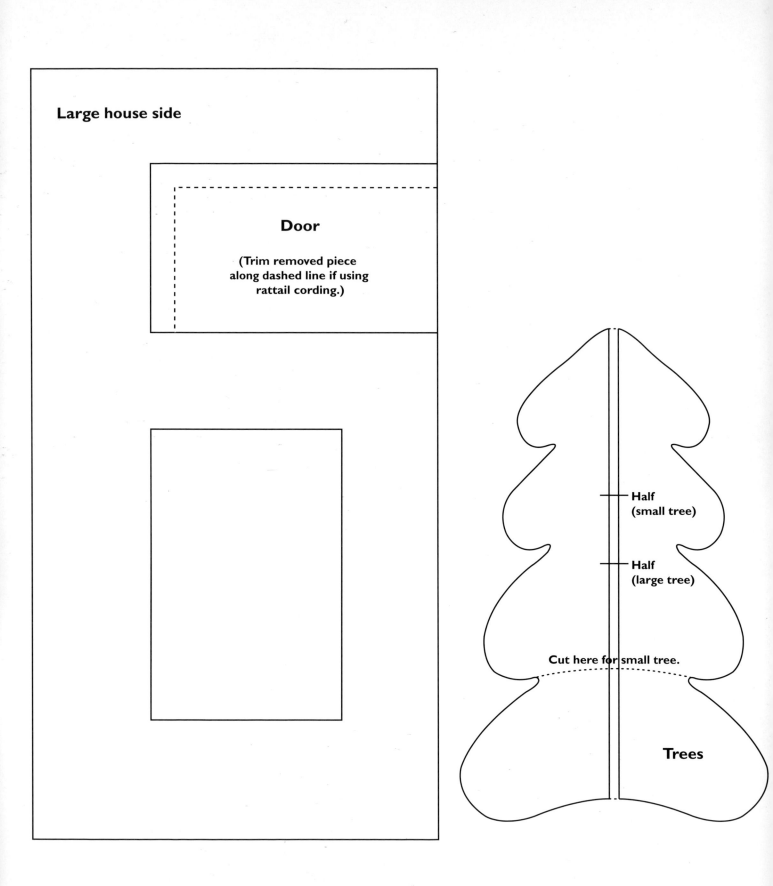

Large house side

Door

(Trim removed piece
along dashed line if using
rattail cording.)

Half
(small tree)

Half
(large tree)

Cut here for small tree.

Trees

sleigh

You won't be able to resist adding a couple of reindeer to this sleigh fit for royalty (or Santa).

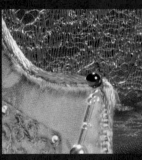

What You'll Need

- ☐ Basic supplies
- ☐ 2 fat quarters of fabric
- ☐ 2½″ × 7″ fabric for the runner spaces, or 4″ × 8″ fabric for the runners
- ☐ 11½″ × 13″ fast2fuse
- ☐ 2½ yards rattail cording
- ☐ 3″ × 12″ Steam-a-Seam 2
- ☐ Embellishments
- ☐ Mini iron—optional, but *very* helpful
- ☐ 1″-wide rotary ruler—optional

How-Tos

sides

1. Fuse your fabrics to each side of an 8″ × 10½″ piece of fast2fuse.

2. Draw 2 sleigh sides (pattern on page 53) on one side of the fused piece and cut them out. **Remember to reverse one side.**

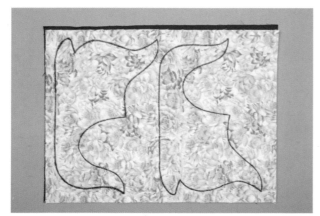

Remember to reverse one side of the sleigh.

fun!

Add any sewing embellishments that you want on the sleigh sides before you fuse the second side of fabric on.

3. On the outside fabric, lightly draw the line for the bottom of the sleigh on each side where the sleigh would connect to the runners. See photo and pattern.

Draw a line on each side for the bottom of the sleigh.
(Drawn darkly for illustration only.)

4. To make the runners show, you can fuse on the spaces between the runners (as shown on page 51), or fuse on the runners themselves from a different fabric. Iron fusible web to a piece of fabric 4″ × 8″ for the runners, or 4″ × 4″ for the spaces. Trace them onto the Steam-a-Seam 2, cut them out, and fuse them on. **Remember to cut one side reversed.**

Cut out the spaces between the runners and fuse them on.

5. Follow the diagram below to sew rattail cording around the edge of each side and along the base of the sleigh. Sew cording around the edges with a 3.0 width, 1.5 length zigzag stitch. Sew the cording on the top edge of the runners (to show the base edge) with a 1.0 width, 1.5 length zigzag stitch, catching just the top edge of the cording. Begin and end with a wide (4.0–5.0 width) zigzag in place, to hold the ends.

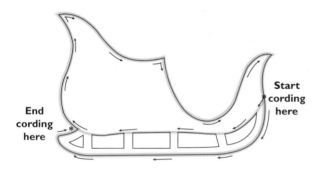

6. Reverse this sewing direction for the other side of the sleigh. Begin at the end point. This keeps the cording on the same side of the piece as you sew.

base

1. Fuse the outside sleigh fabric to one side of a 3½″ × 13″ piece of fast2fuse.

2. Trim the fused piece to 2¾″ wide.

3. Cut a 5″ × 13″ piece of fabric for the inside of the sleigh.

4. Center the fast2fuse on the fabric and fuse it in place.

5. Trim the edges of the fabric to 1″ from the sides of the fast2fuse.

Trim the edges of the fabric to 1″.

6. Follow the manufacturer's directions and fuse a 1″ strip of Steam-a-Seam2 to the extra fabric at the edge of the fast2fuse.

7. Sew rattail cording to one end of the base. Remember to begin and end with a wider anchoring zigzag stitch. Trim the cording flush with the sides of the base.

8. Take the paper off the Steam-a-Seam 2 and clip the fabric on each side every ½″.

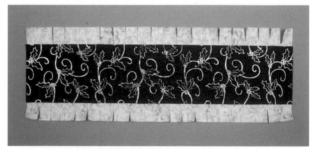

Clip each side every ½″.

9. Start at the back of the sleigh with the end that has rattail cording on it, and pin the base to the side by pushing pins straight into the side and into the edge of the base. Line up the base with the top edge of the runners (see page 52).

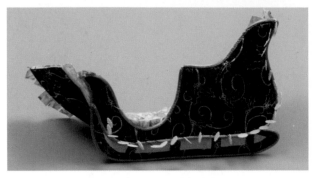

Pin the base to the sides.

10. Gently overlap the clipped edges as you pin the base in, and press them firmly once the side is pinned. Do not iron them yet.

11. Pin the second side the same way.

NOTE

The base will be longer than the sides of the sleigh—that is built into the pattern, since everyone will pin slightly differently. When you get all but about 1½″ of the second side pinned, unpin an equal amount of the first side and trim the base evenly across the front end of the sleigh. Sew a piece of rattail cording across the end and finish pinning. Begin repinning from the end of the base back toward the middle of the sleigh if you have any unevenness.

Trim the end of the base and add rattail cording.

12. Trim the clipped edges to the shape of the sleigh where necessary (at the front and back end, and at the step-in).

13. Iron the clipped edges firmly to the sides of the sleigh. A mini iron really helps with this.

14. Put a line of dimensional glitter paint where the sides and base come together on the outside of the sleigh.

seat

1. Cut a 3″ × 2⅝″ piece of fast2fuse.

2. Fuse it to the center of a 3″ × 6″ piece of fabric, placing the long sides parallel. This can be the same fabric as the inside base, or it can be a different fabric.

3. Trim the long sides flush with the fast2fuse. Leave 1″ of fabric at each end.

easy!

Decoratively trim the seat fabric where it will iron onto the sleigh.

4. Sew rattail cording to the long sides of the seat. At the beginning and end, tack a short length behind the extra fabric on the ends.

5. Fuse Steam-a-Seam 2 to the 1″ of extra fabric on the ends. Place the paper-backed ends face to face and iron the piece in half to make a crease for the edge of the seat. Add any sewing embellishments at this point.

Seat ready to install

6. Place the seat into the sleigh. Be sure you like the placement, remove the paper backing, and then fuse it in place.

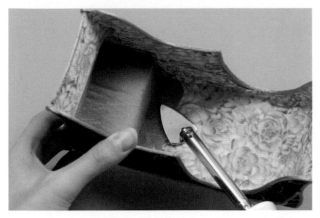

Fuse the seat in place. A mini iron makes this much easier.

fun!

You can fussy cut some fabric or lace to fuse in and cover the edges of this fabric if they show more than you like.

7. Outline the runner spaces with dimensional glitter paint and do any additional beading or embellishing you want.

Variation

I added free-motion stitching in gold thread, fused on gold lace, and added lots of jingle bells to embellish this holiday sleigh

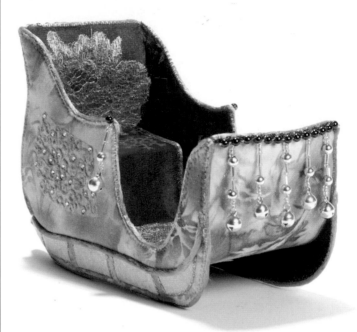

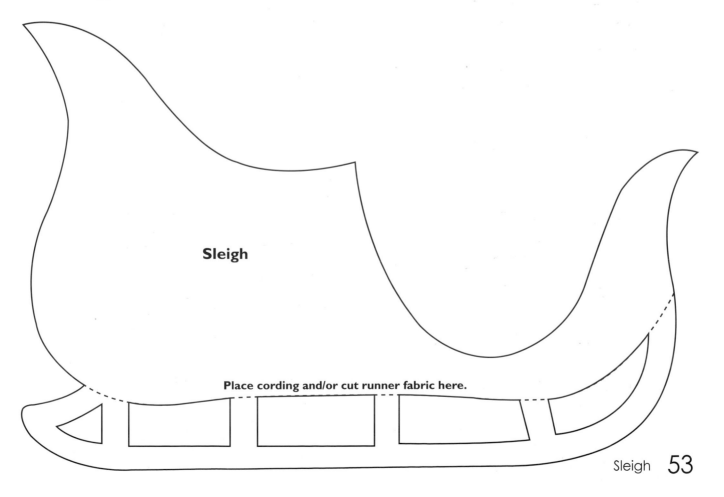

Sleigh

Place cording and/or cut runner fabric here.

3-dimensional advent calendar & ornaments

Put this on your table and everyone will know just when Christmas is coming!

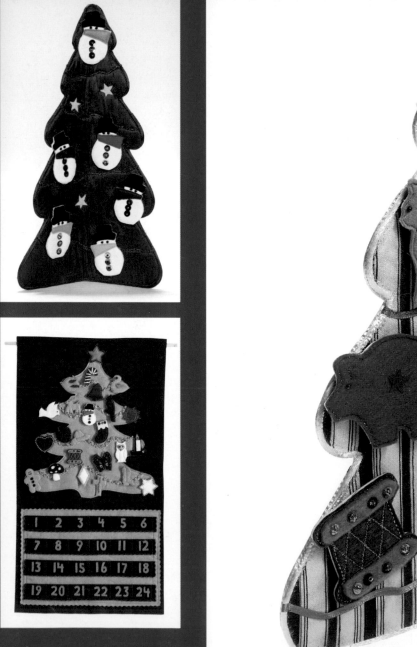

What You'll Need

- Basic supplies
- 11″ × 22″ fast2fuse and felt or fabric for the tree
- Large scraps fast2fuse for the ornaments
- Assorted felt scraps for the ornaments
- ½ yard fabric for the ornament backs

- 3½ yards rattail cording for the tree
- 3 yards decorative cord, yarn, ribbon, or ⅛″-wide fusible ribbon for trim
- 18″ of ¾″-wide hook-and-loop tape (This fabric should show markings easily.) (Choose a color to complement your tree.)
- Embellishments for the ornaments

How-Tos

tree

1. Trace 3 tree sides (pattern on page 62) onto the fast2fuse.

Draw the tree pattern 3 times on the fast2fuse.

2. Fuse fabric or felt to the *unmarked* side of the fast2fuse.

NOTE

I like the look and feel of felt for the tree; however, it takes longer and requires more pressure to fuse it to the fast2fuse. With synthetic felt, be careful of the iron temperature, and with wool felt, be patient—it will take time to get the heat through it.

3. Cut out the tree sides. Make sure your pattern is correct and that you cut carefully. You will be sewing these pieces back to back so the edges will need to match very well. You will not need fabric on the back sides of these pieces.

4. Use polyester monofilament thread to zigzag rattail cording around each piece (pages 10–11). I like to start and end at the bottom of the tree.

5. With a wide zigzag, couch decorative cord, yarn, or ribbon on with the monofilament thread. Fusible ribbon (I like Hot Ribbon) or ⅛″ double-faced satin ribbon both work well here also. Follow your bliss—it's your tree! Fold the beginning and end over to the back of the piece and sew it down with your first stitches. This eliminates having to pin or hold the ends when you sew the pieces together.

fun!

Make each side different, and fill one side with ornaments before you turn the tree to fill the next. It will look like a different tree every 8 days.

6. Cut out and sew 8 small circles, stars, or squares of the hook side of the hook-and-loop tape onto each of the 3 sides of the tree (24 total). I use polyester monofilament in the bobbin and the needle for applying both the hook-and-loop tape and ribbon.

NOTE
I found unusual colors of hook-and-loop tape at our local outdoor activewear fabric store.

One side of the tree with the ribbon and hook-and-loop tape sewn on

fast!

Make a felt tree and put the hook part of the hook-and-loop tape on the ornaments instead. They will stick to the felt without the small circles or stars. However, this would not work well for households with children who like to reposition the ornaments frequently.

fun!

Put 8 pieces of hook-and-loop tape on one side, and 7 and 9 on the other 2 sides.

7. Place 2 sides of the tree back to back. Use a narrow (2.0 width, 1.5 length) zigzag and sew over the same stitches that hold the rattail cording on. Sew from the center of the treetop to just around the corner on the bottom of the tree. Leave the base open for storage of the ornaments.

8. Lightly steam out some of the center wrinkles by putting your hand inside and ironing with steam. Hold the tree while it cools.

easy!

Make a small, simple cloth bag for the ornaments. You can keep it inside the tree and lift the tree to pull out a new ornament for the day.

fast!

Spray the whole tree with Fabric Glitter Spray for extra glitz. (See Resources on page 63.)

Or, make your ornaments, place them on the tree, and enjoy the anticipation of Christmas.

Angel

Candle

Diamond

Gift box

Pear

Apple

Candy cane

Dog

Gingerbread boy

Pig

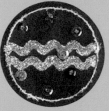

Ball

Cat

Dove—flying

Heart

Reindeer

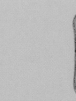

Bell

Christmas stocking

Dove—stylized

Holly leaves

Snowflake

Blue jay/Cardinal

Cowboy boot

Drum

Mushroom

Snowman

Butterfly

Cowboy hat

Duck

Owl

Star

ornaments

1. Trace and cut out the patterns (pages 60–61) for the ornaments you want to make.

2. Sort these by the color of background you want on them. For example, you can use red for the apple, heart, cardinal, and candy cane, or white for the snowman, doves, and mushroom.

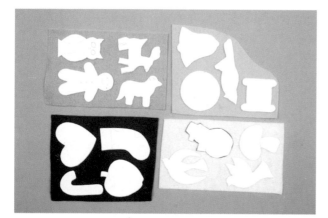

Sort ornaments by background color.

3. Cut a piece of fast2fuse the size you need for all the ornaments that you want of the same color.

4. Iron a piece of backing fabric to the entire piece. This fabric will not show.

5. Trace the ornaments on the backing fabric. Remember to reverse them from the direction you want them to face.

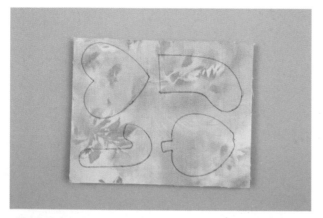

Trace the ornaments for one color felt on the backing fabric.

6. Sew a ½˝ length of hook-and-loop tape to the center of each of the drawn ornaments. The easiest way to do this is by machine, using a stiletto to hold the hook-and-loop tape in place for the first few stitches. Sew them on with an × across the square, or sew around the edges—I'd do this free-motion! If you prefer, you can sew them on by hand. Remember to sew the fuzzy side of the hook-and-loop tape to the ornaments—the hooks are on the tree.

fast!

Cut most of your small pieces of hook-and-loop tape before you start sewing so that they are ready for you.

7. Iron the color of felt for these ornaments (red or white in our examples) to the other side of the fast2fuse. Use a protective cloth or paper over the felt if you want to retain its fuzzy nap.

8. Sew around the tracing of the ornament from the back side with decorative thread in the bobbin.

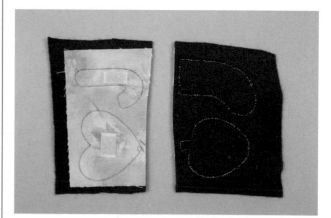

Iron the background felt to the front side and sew around the lines from the back.

9. Cut out the individual ornaments just outside the sewing line and embellish them as desired.

10. When adding other decorative felt pieces, you can cut them out and glue or sew them on, or you can place them on the front of the ornament, turn it over, sew around the lines where you want the new color, turn it back over, and trim away the excess.

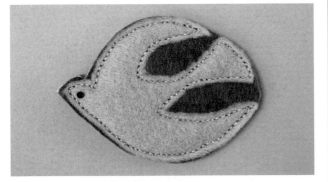

Sew a new color from the back and trim around it, or sew/glue a shaped piece on top for additional embellishment.

easy!

Finish the edges of these ornaments with either dimensional paint or rattail cording if you don't want the fast2fuse to show.

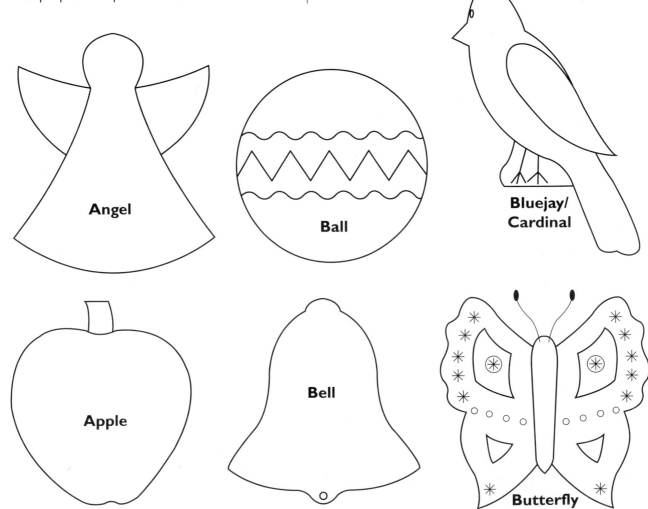

Angel

Ball

Bluejay/ Cardinal

Apple

Bell

Butterfly

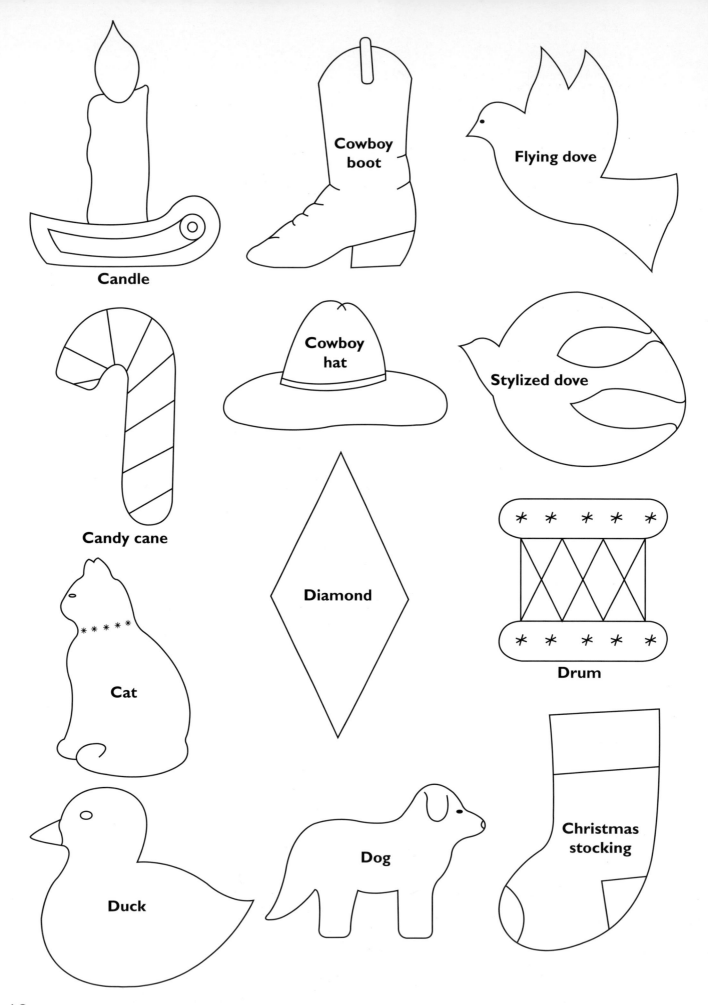

Candle

Cowboy boot

Flying dove

Candy cane

Cowboy hat

Stylized dove

Cat

Diamond

Drum

Duck

Dog

Christmas stocking

Gift box

Mushroom

Reindeer

Gingerbread boy

Owl

Snowflake

Heart

Pear

Snowman

5-pointed star

Pig

Holly leaves

Advent tree

Resources

Supplies

A Common Thread
Email: actbernina@aol.com
www.acommonthreadfabrics.com
Quilting supplies

Bo-Nash (North America) Inc.
800-527-8811
www.bonash.com
Fusible powder

C&T Publishing
800-284-1114
www.ctpub.com

fast2fuse interfacing: regular and heavyweight

28"-wide double-sided fusible stiff interfacing

Cotton Patch Mail Order
800-835-4418
Email: quiltusa@yahoo.com
www.quiltusa.com
Quilting supplies

Duncan Enterprises
800-438-6226
www.duncancrafts.com

Aleene's Jewel-It and Stop Fraying, Tulip Fabric Glitter Spray, dimensional fashion paint, and iron-on crystals

Freudenberg–Pellon
800-331-6509
www.ShopPellon.com
Wonder Under: Pellon transfer web #805
Available at most quilt and sewing stores.

Glitz & Glamour
800-576-6755, code 4
www.glitzandglamour.net
Iron-on crystals, studs, and motifs

Imagination International
866-662-6742
Hot ribbon and fusible ribbon

Kandi
800-985-2634
www.kandicorp.com
L'orna Decorative Touch Wand & Swarovski hot-fix crystals

OESD Oklahoma Embroidery Supply & Design
www.oesd.com

Isacord Thread: Large spools carry 1,000 meters. Small spools are sold as Mettler Polysheen, with 200 meters.

EZ Glitzer and Swarovski hot-fix crystals

Prym Consumer USA, Inc.
800-255-7796
www.dritz.com
Omnigrid products, Fray Check, and 3/4" plastic rings for hanging the wreath

Timber Lane Press
800-752-3353
Email: qltblox@earthlink.net
www.timtexstore.com
Timtex: 22"-wide yardage; a bolt holds 10 yards

Also available through major quilting supply distributors and your local quilt store.

Trimtex
570-326-9135
www.trimtex.com
Cording

Fabric

Classic Cottons
www.classiccottons.com

Johansen Dyeworks
www.lindajohansen.com
Hand-dyed fabrics

RJR Fabrics
www.rjrfabrics.com

Robert Kauffman Fabrics
www.robertkaufman.com

Timeless Treasures
www.ttfabrics.com

About the Author

Linda Johansen is the author of four other Fast, Fun & Easy books featuring three-dimensional construction. In her spare time she is an award-winning quilter, a fabric dyer, and a gardener. She has one son in college in Philadelphia (Haverford) and one son and his wife moving to north central Washington. Add two dogs, one gran-dog-ger, a grand-puppy on the way, and a very patient, supportive husband, and she is happy. Linda lives with varying combinations of the above in Corvallis, Oregon.

Great Titles
from C&T PUBLISHING